Birds of Paradise

A Coloring Expedition

Edwin Scholes
Tim Laman
Andrew Leach

The**Cornell**Lab of Ornithology

Designed by Hans Teensma, Impress, and Patricia N Gonzalez

Library of Congress Cataloging-in-Publication Data available.

ISBN: 978-1943645-38-1

Manufactured in China

10 9 8 7 6 5 4 3 2 1

Produced by the
Cornell Lab Publishing Group
120A North Salem Street
Apex, NC 27502

www.CornellLabPG.com

By buying products with the FSC label you are
supporting the growth of responsible forest
management worldwide.

FSC
www.fsc.org

MIX
Paper from
responsible sources
FSC® C124385

Acknowledgments

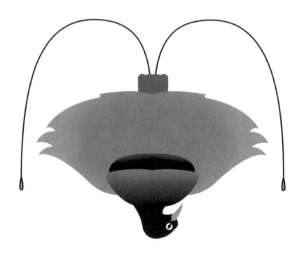

We thank the Cornell Lab of Ornithology and its constituency for supporting the Birds-of-Paradise Project. We thank the many individuals and organizations that have enabled us to see, study and photograph birds-of-paradise through the years. We thank the many colleagues and collaborators for the comments, insights, and support needed to complete this book, especially Mary Guthrie, Mya Thompson, Miyoko Chu, Diane Tessaglia-Hymes, Hans Teensma, and Mike Webster. We offer sincere thanks to Brian Scott Sockin for helping to create the opportunity that made this book possible at every step along the way. As always, we thank our families and friends for their support: Kim Bostwick, Nolan Scholes, Natalie Scholes, Cheryl Knott, Russel Laman, Jessica Laman, Madeline Seiler, and Stiles Seiler.

About Birds-of-Paradise

WHAT MAKES the 39 species of birds-of-paradise so extraordinary, so unlike most other birds? Two immediate characteristics that stand out are shape and color. It is the glorious extremes to which evolution has pushed the boundaries of possibility with respect to the shape and color of feathers, body postures, skin patches, eyes, whole appendages such as legs and wings, and even the insides of their mouths. Virtually every feature has been transformed to an extreme of shape, color, or both.

Found throughout forested habitats, from lowland swamps to montane cloud forests, all over the island of New Guinea, nearby islands, and part of northeastern Australia, the birds-of-paradise are some of the greatest beauties in the natural world. The beauty of the birds-of-paradise ranges from the abstract to the absurd; if it didn't exist in the natural world, it would be difficult to imagine. Yet it would not be wrong to say the "artist" whose keen eye has crafted these fantastic creatures is Mother Nature herself.

In this case, beauty was shaped by female birds-of-paradise, whose individual preferences for mates have cumulatively selected fathers for their offspring based on the colors they find most pleasing, the ornaments they find most attractive, and the dances they find most desirable. The features that we humans find so appealing among the male birds-of-paradise are outcomes of thousands of years of evolution through the process of sexual selection.

The resulting diversity of color, shape, and form is nothing short of astonishing: from deep crimson to penetrating electric blue, from firework-like bursts of plumes to bizarre geometric abstractions that defy characterization. It's a riotous symphony of shape and color, all choreographed and executed with unbelievable precision and dexterity. These traits are why the birds-of-paradise are so rewarding to observe and study, and why the Cornell Lab of Ornithology is committed to conserving their future through the Birds-of-Paradise Project.

To explore the world of the birds-of-paradise is to explore the extremes of shape and color and to investigate the boundaries connecting natural beauty and wonder. By tracing the beautiful outlines of their shapes as drawn by artist Andrew Leach and infusing them with color inspired by the photos of Tim Laman, you are, in a sense, reenacting the process of aesthetic evolution that has been played out in forests of New Guinea for thousands of years. Your hand is the hand of female choice directing the evolution of the birds-of-paradise.

We hope that your artistic process will be fun and stimulating, and give you a tangible connection to these birds through your exploration of the very things that make them so extraordinary— their shape and color.

—E. S.

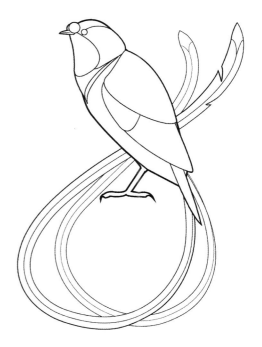

Ribbon-tailed Astrapia

Astrapia mayeri

The male Ribbon-tailed Astrapia has a beaming white tail three times as long as his body. Although the brilliant blue-green iridescent plumage on his head and throat is less conspicuous at first, it is equally impressive when viewed up close.

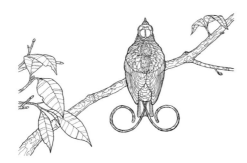

Wilson's Bird-of-Paradise
Cicinnurus respublica

He may be small, but the male Wilson's Bird-of-Paradise is striking and colorful. They are the embodiment of ornamental extremes, with curled tail feathers and a skullcap of bare blue skin. They live only on two islands off of western New Guinea, where males clear and maintain display "courts" on the ground.

Crinkle-collared Manucode

Manucodia chalybatus

The Crinkle-collared Manucode can often be found searching for figs, a favored fruit. Its name comes from the "crinkled" feathers on its neck, but they are rarely visible from a distance.

Pale-billed Sicklebill

Drepanornis bruijnii

One of the least-ornamented birds-of-paradise, the male Pale-billed Sicklebill's most distinctive features are the patch of bare facial skin and the iridescent-tipped feathers on his breast, which form a small pectoral fan. Exactly how these ornaments are used remains a mystery.

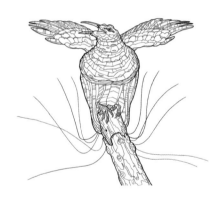

Twelve-wired Bird-of-Paradise
Seleucidis melanoleucus

Vocalizing in the dawn mist, a male Twelve-wired Bird-of-Paradise calls for a mate from his favored display site, a bare branch rising vertically above the surrounding swamp forest. When a female arrives, he will swipe the unusual wiry ends of his yellow plumes back and forth across her upper body.

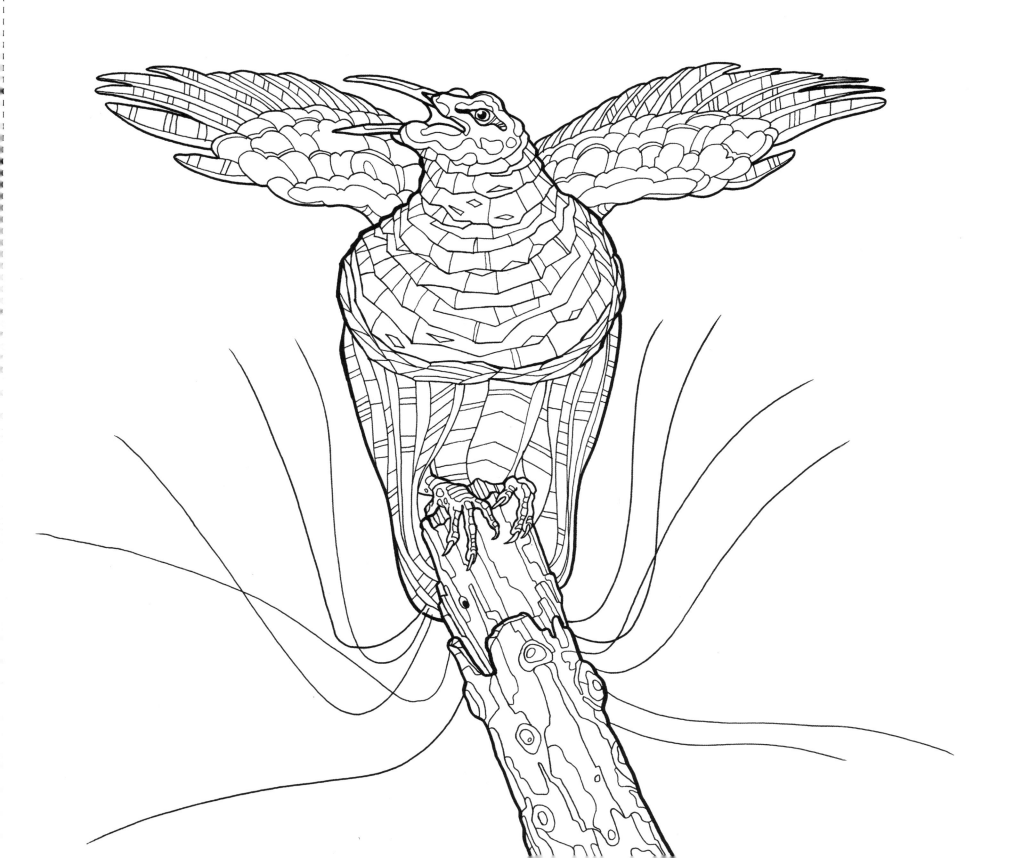

King of Saxony Bird-of-Paradise
Pteridophora alberti

With two antenna-like plumes sprouting from his head, the
male King of Saxony Bird-of-Paradise is a feathered wonder.
His rhythmic bouncing display is an extraordinary sight, and
his calls, which sound something like radio static, are an iconic
sound of New Guinea's montane forests.

Raggiana Bird-of-Paradise

Paradisaea raggiana

Performing the "flower pose," the male Raggiana Bird-of-Paradise turns away from the female with his head downward so that the plumes from his flanks fall like flower petals over his back. A female watching from behind is engulfed in a mass of rich color and texture.

Wahnes's Parotia

Parotia wahnesi

Found only in a narrow band of forest in the Huon Peninsula of northeastern New Guinea, Wahnes's Parotia has the longest tail of any parotia. He uses a cleared patch of ground, a "display court," to perform for females, who observe from a horizontal perch above.

Huon Astrapia

Astrapia rothschildi

The Huon Astrapia is one of the least-known birds-of-paradise. The male performs an upside-down display in which he wields his long paddle-shaped tail like a banner.

Greater Bird-of-Paradise

Paradisaea apoda

With the yellow plumes from his flanks cascading over his back in an explosion of color, the male Greater Bird-of-Paradise shows why his feathers have been treasured by plume hunters for centuries. One of the largest members of the family, this species is also one of the most iconic.

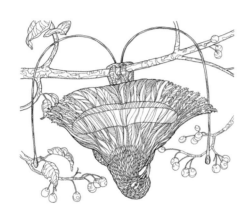

Blue Bird-of-Paradise

Paradisaea rudolphi

Many consider the Blue Bird-of-Paradise to be the most beautiful of all, with dazzling blue feathers seeming to radiate from within. The male's intense color and bizarre shape when hanging upside down during display are a wonder to behold.

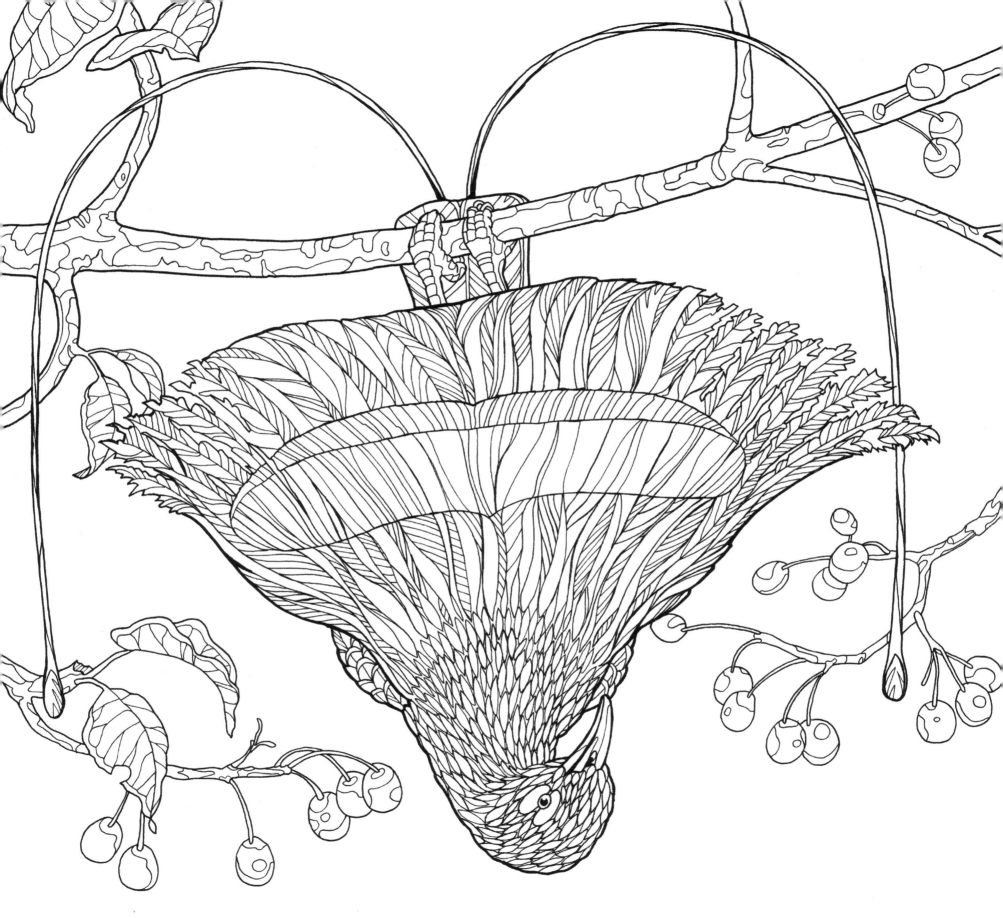

Bronze Parotia

Parotia berlepschi

Sunlight radiates down through a gap in the forest canopy
and catches the black feathers on the back of the male Bronze
Parotia. In this light the feathers glimmer with the bronze hue
that gives him his name.

Trumpet Manucode

Phonygammus keraudrenii

The Trumpet Manucode has a broad elevational range, from lowland rainforests to mountain cloud forests. Like most birds-of-paradise, its diet is primarily fruit; this species consumes a higher proportion of figs than other birds-of-paradise.

Magnificent Riflebird

Ptiloris magnificus

When a female is near, the male Magnificent Riflebird transforms into a fantastic black ovoid shape by spreading his wings widely. He whips his head vigorously from side to side while moving his body up and down in the rhythm of his display.

Red Bird-of-Paradise

Paradisaea rubra

As daylight breaks, sunlight reaches the leafy canopy of a
towering forest tree. A male Red Bird-of-Paradise turns his
body, wings open, to face downward from a bare branch.
His flank plumes catch the light and his body is framed by the
heart-shaped ribbons cascading from his tail.

Paradise Riflebird

Ptiloris paradiseus

When displaying, the male Paradise Riflebird stands upright and lifts his wings over his head. He performs a rhythmic "fan dance," alternately moving each spread wing from side to side while hiding his head behind them.

Glossy-mantled Manucode

Manucodia ater

The name of the Glossy-mantled Manucode comes from the smooth, glossy sheen sometimes visible on its upper back. Like all the manucodes, males and females look alike.

Stephanie's Astrapia

Astrapia stephaniae

Probing a cluster of schefflera fruits, the male Stephanie's
Astrapia pries individual fruits free and tosses them down his
throat. From a perch at the edge of the cloud forest, his brilliant
metallic blue-green throat sparkles with each turn of his head.

Carola's Parotia

Parotia carolae

As he shuffles forward and back along his court, the male Carola's Parotia positions himself beneath a perch where females watch from above. He bows down and lifts up with his feathered "skirt" wrapped around his body.

Lesser Bird-of-Paradise

Paradisaea minor

With plumes that glow in the sunlight, the male Lesser Bird-of-Paradise calls to attract the attention of rivals and potential mates. Although a male occasionally displays alone, he usually displays with other males in a communal courtship location shared by multiple males, a "lek tree."

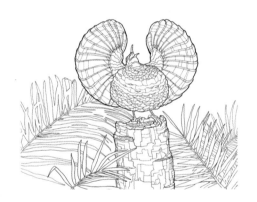

Victoria's Riflebird

Ptiloris victoriae

His blunt-tipped wing feathers unfurled, the male Victoria's Riflebird reveals how female mating preferences have altered wing shape to form an ornament at the expense of aerodynamics. While displaying, he raises his rounded wings over his head, facing the female on his tree-stump display pole.

Black-billed Sicklebill

Drepanornis albertisi

Clinging to the trunk of a small tree, the male Black-billed Sicklebill leans back until his body is perpendicular to the trunk. Lifting his flank plumes around himself, he undergoes a radical transformation into an unusual flat disc-like form.

Brown Sicklebill

Epimachus meyeri

With a long saber-like tail and decurved bill, the male Brown Sicklebill is an impressive sight. His voice is as impressive as his appearance—a powerful, hollow burst, like a machine gun firing in the distance.

Western Parotia

Parotia sefilata

From a secretive stage on the forest floor that he has cleared of leaves, the male Western Parotia transforms into a little skirt-clad dancer. The "skirt" consists of flared upper breast and flank feathers, a display evolved for the sole purpose of attracting a mate.

Splendid Astrapia

Astrapia splendidissima

The male Splendid Astrapia may have the shortest tail among the "long-tailed" birds-of-paradise, but he has the distinction of being the most iridescently feathered. In fact, he is one of the most iridescent birds in the world.

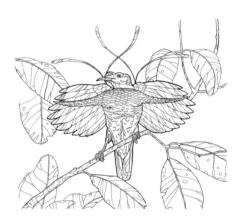

Standardwing Bird-of-Paradise

Semioptera wallacii

Although perhaps not the most beautiful bird-of-paradise, the male standardwing can claim the distinction of being one of the most bizarre. What would normally be tiny feathers on the top of the wing have been elaborated into flaglike "standards" through the power of sexual selection, driven by the females' preferences for these ornaments.

Curl-crested Manucode

Manucodia comrii

With crests of frizzled feathers, male and female Curl-crested Manucodes look alike. Unlike most birds-of-paradise, both parents are thought to attend the nest and help care for the chicks.

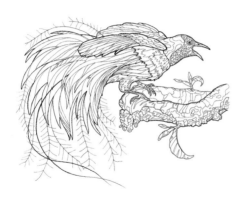

Emperor Bird-of-Paradise

Paradisaea guilielmi

The flank plumes of the male Emperor Bird-of-Paradise are sparsely filamented and whiter than those of the other Paradisaea species. Most striking is how, during the peak of their display, several males in close proximity to one another simultaneously hang upside-down.

Jobi Manucode

Manucodia jobiensis

Nearly indistinguishable from the Crinkle-collared and Glossy-mantled manucodes, the Jobi Manucode is best identified by its voice. Unfortunately, this species also tends to be rather silent, which makes identification difficult.

Superb Bird-of-Paradise

Lophorina superba

A master of manipulation, the male Superb Bird-of-Paradise uses the feathered "cape" at the back of his head, his iridescent crown patch, and the elongated feathers on his breast to perform the most fantastical courtship display of any bird in the world.

Long-tailed Paradigalla

Paradigalla carunculata

Known only from the Arfak Mountains of western New Guinea, the Long-tailed Paradigalla is unusual in that both sexes look alike. They earned the name "paradise chicken" (paradigalla) because their fleshy facial wattles resemble those of a chicken.

King Bird-of-Paradise

Cicinnurus regius

The male King Bird-of-Paradise is one of the smallest birds-of-paradise, but what he lacks in size he makes up for in color. His crimson head and brilliant white undersides contrast sharply with the emerald green feathers of his breast and the tips of his tail.

Paradise-crow

Lycocorax pyrrhopterus

Not as ornate as its relatives, the Paradise-crow is the most crowlike member of the family and hints at what the common ancestor of the birds-of-paradise might have looked like.

Lawes's Parotia

Parotia lawesii

A male Lawes's Parotia grabs a brightly colored capsule fruit from a favorite feeding tree. His six long wire-like feathers sway behind him, and the iridescent feathers on his breast shimmer and sparkle with every movement.

Magnificent Bird-of-Paradise

Cicinnurus magnificus

The male Magnificent Bird-of-Paradise has a comical array of ornamental features. His tail is curled like a metallic handlebar mustache. His legs are blue and his breast is green. Although often hidden, the feathers at the back of his neck can be flipped up to form a glowing yellow halo.

Arfak Astrapia

Astrapia nigra

Rotating tail first to hang upside down, the male Arfak Astrapia fans his flag-like tail. Inverted, his brilliant green undersides create a surprising combination of color and shape for the female to observe from above.

Short-tailed Paradigalla
Paradigalla bevicauda

Stocky and black, the Short-tailed Paradigalla's most defining feature is the fleshy yellow wattles that cover its face. This is one of the few birds-of-paradise in which both sexes look alike.

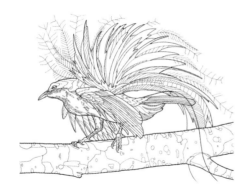

Goldie's Bird-of-Paradise

Paradisaea decora

The most spectacular part of the Goldie's Bird-of-Paradise display is how two males perform in choreographed synchrony. Their ritual begins with idiosyncratic calling, but their voices become increasingly synchronized until suddenly they burst into a head-down display while performing an extraordinary duet.

Black Sicklebill

Epimachus fastosus

The male Black Sicklebill perches upright on a pole-like tree stump during display. He fans his odd breast plumes around his head, transforming into a bizarre, almost sinister-looking ovoid form framed and highlighted by a thin blue line.

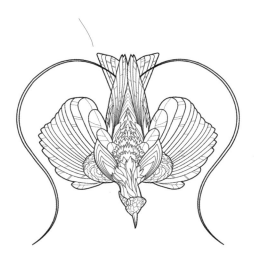

The Cornell Lab of Ornithology is a world leader in the study, appreciation, and conservation of birds. Founded in 1915, the Cornell Lab engages tens of millions of people worldwide each year in learning more about birds and their natural environments. The Lab's work is made possible with support from people who care about nature. Join as a member to help the birds, and you'll receive a subscription to the Lab's beautiful magazine, *Living Bird*. Visit birds.cornell.edu/join.

The Birds of Paradise
39 Species

Ribbon-tailed Astrapia

Page 6

Wilson's Bird-of-Paradise

Page 8

Crinkle-collared Manucode

Page 10

Pale-billed Sicklebill

Page 12

Twelve-wired Bird-of-Paradise

Page 14

King of Saxony Bird-of-Paradise

Page 16

Raggianna Bird-of-Paradise

Page 18

Wahnes's Parotia

Page 20

Huon Astrapia
Page 22

Greater Bird-of-Paradise
Page 24

Blue Bird-of-Paradise
Page 26

Bronze Parotia
Page 28

Trumpet Manucode
Page 30

Magnificent Riflebird
Page 32

Red Bird-of-Paradise
Page 34

Paradise Riflebird
Page 36

Glossy-mantled Manucode
Page 38

Stephanie's Astrapia
Page 40

Carola's Parotia
Page 42

Lesser Bird-of-Paradise
Page 44

Victoria's Riflebird
Page 46

Black-billed Sicklebill
Page 48

Brown Sicklebill
Page 50

Western Parotia
Page 52

Splendid Astrapia
Page 54

Standardwing Bird-of-Paradise
Page 56

Curl-crested Manucode
Page 58

Emperor Bird-of-Paradise
Page 60

Jobi Manucode
Page 62

Superb Bird-of-Paradise
Page 64

Long-tailed Paradigalla
Page 66

King Bird-of-Paradise
Page 68

Paradise-crow
Page 70

Lawes's Parotia
Page 72

Magnificent Bird-of-Paradise
Page 74

Arfak Astrapia
Page 76

Short-tailed Paradigalla
Page 78

Goldie's Bird-of-Paradise
Page 80

Black Sicklebill
Page 82

Watch the awe-inspiring Birds-of-Paradise Project Introduction Video from the Cornell Lab on YouTube, viewed more than 11 million times!

Find it on the **LabofOrnithology** Channel on YouTube, or type the URL **bit.ly/1q3kIR7** directly into your browser.